The
WORST-CASE
SCENARIO®

Little Book for Survival

Josh

Kansas City

06 07 08 09 10 WKT 10 9 8 7 6 5 4 3 2 1

ISBN-13: 978-0-7407-6176-8
ISBN-10: 0-7407-6176-5

Library of Congress Control Number: 2006924942

Published under license from Chronicle Books, LLC.
Based on the book THE WORST-CASE SCENARIO®
Survival Handbook by Joshua Piven and David Borgenicht,
© 1999 by Quirk Productions, Inc. Worst-Case Scenario®
and The Worst-Case Scenario Survival Handbook™ are
trademarks of Quirk Productions, Inc. First published by
Chronicle Books, LLC, San Francisco, California, U.S.A.

www.andrewsmcmeel.com

WARNING

When a life is imperiled or a dire situation is at hand, safe alternatives may not exist. To deal with the worst-case scenarios presented in this book, we highly recommend—insist, actually—that the best course of action is to consult a professionally trained expert. DO NOT ATTEMPT TO UNDERTAKE ANY OF THE ACTIVITIES DESCRIBED IN THIS BOOK YOURSELF.

THE PUBLISHER, AUTHORS, AND EXPERTS DISCLAIM ANY

CONTENTS

Preface . . . viii

PREFACE

Anything that can go wrong will.

—**Murphy's Law**

Be prepared.

—**Boy Scout motto**

The principle behind this book is a simple one: You just never know.

You never really know what curves life will throw at you, what is lurking around the corner, what is hovering above, what is swimming beneath the surface. You never know when you might be called upon to perform an act of extreme bravery and to choose life or death with your own actions. But when you are called, we want to be sure that you know what to do.

The information in this book comes directly from dozens of expert sources—stuntmen, physicians, EMT instructors, survival experts, alligator farmers, marine biologists, bullfighters, and avalanche-rescue-patrol members, to name a few. Within this book, you will find simple, step-by-step instructions for dealing with twenty-one life- and limb-threatening situations, with instructive illustrations throughout.

So keep this pocket-size book on hand at all times. It is informative and entertaining, but useful, too. Because you just never know.

CHAPTER 1

GREAT ESCAPES AND ENTRANCES

HOW TO ESCAPE
FROM QUICKSAND

1 When walking in quicksand country, always carry a stout pole.
As you start to sink, lay the pole on the surface and flop your back onto it in a floating position.

2 Move slowly.
Do not struggle. Quicksand is not difficult to float in—but it can suck you down if you struggle against it.

great escapes and entrances

When in an area with quicksand, bring a stout pole and use it to put your back into a floating position.

Place the pole at a right angle from your spine to keep your hips afloat.

3. | *great escapes and entrances*

3 Place the pole at a right angle to your spine to keep your hips afloat. Slowly, pull out one leg, then the other.

4 Take the shortest route to firmer ground, moving slowly.

HOW TO BREAK DOWN A DOOR

 Give the door a well-placed kick or two to the lock area to break it down. Running at the door and slamming against it with your shoulder or body is not usually as effective as kicking with your foot. Your foot exerts more force than your shoulder, and you will be able to direct this force toward the area of the locking mechanism more effectively with your foot.

5. | *great escapes and entrances*

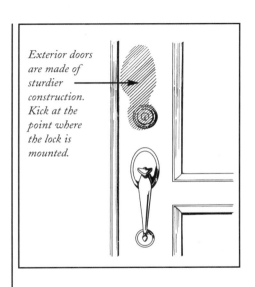

Exterior doors are made of sturdier construction. Kick at the point where the lock is mounted.

HOW TO BREAK INTO A CAR WITH A HANGER

1 Take a wire hanger and bend it into a long J.

2 Square off the bottom of the J so the square is 1½ to 2 inches wide.

3 Slide the hanger into the door, between the window and the weather stripping.

7. *great escapes and entrances*

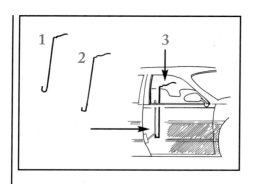

Open the door by feel and by trial and error. Feel for the end of the button rod and, when you have it, pull it up to open the lock.

HOW TO ESCAPE FROM A SINKING CAR

1 If possible, open the window as soon as you hit the water.

Escape through the window and swim to the surface.

2 Alternatively, try breaking the window with your foot or a heavy object, such as an antitheft steering wheel lock.

3 As a last resort, wait until the car begins filling with water, and then make your escape.

Do not panic. When the water level reaches your head, take a deep breath and hold it. Now the pressure should be equalized inside and outside the car, and you should be able to open the door and swim to the surface.

CHAPTER 2

THE BEST DEFENSE

HOW TO ESCAPE
FROM A BEAR

1 Lie still and quiet.
Documented attacks show that an
attack by a mother black bear often
ends when the person stops fighting.

2 Stay where you are and do not climb a
tree to escape the bear.
Black bears can climb trees quickly
and easily and will come after you.
The odds are that the bear will leave
you alone if you stay put.

12. *the best defense*

3 If you are lying still and the bear attacks, strike back with anything you can. Go for the bear's eyes or its snout.

While all bears are dangerous, these three situations render even more of a threat.

Bears habituated to human food.

Bears defending a fresh kill.

Females protecting cubs.

HOW TO
ESCAPE FROM A
MOUNTAIN LION

1 Try to make yourself appear bigger by opening your coat.
The lion is less likely to attack a larger animal.

2 If the lion still behaves aggressively, throw stones.
Convince the lion you are not prey.

14. *the best defense*

3 If you are attacked, fight back.
Most mountain lions are small enough
that an average-size human can ward off
an attack. Do not curl up and play dead.

*If you see a
mountain lion,
open your coat to
make yourself
appear larger.*

the best defense

HOW TO FEND OFF AN ALLIGATOR

1 Cover the alligator's eyes.
This will usually make it more sedate.

2 If you are attacked, go for the eyes and nose.
Use any weapon you have, or your fist.

3 If its jaws are closed on something you
want to remove (for example, a limb),
tap or punch the alligator on the snout
or behind the ears.
Alligators often open their mouths

16. *the best defense*

when tapped lightly. Do not allow the alligator to shake you or roll over, which will cause severe tissue damage.

4 Seek medical attention immediately, even for a small cut or bruise. Alligators have a huge number of pathogens in their mouths.

To get an alligator to release something it has in its mouth, tap it on the snout.

the best defense

HOW TO DEAL WITH A CHARGING BULL

1 Look for an escape route, cover, or high ground.

Bulls can easily outrun humans. Don't run unless you see an open door, a fence to jump, or another safe haven.

2 Remove your shirt or hat.

Use this to distract the bull. It does not matter what color the clothing is. Despite the colors bullfighters tradi-tionally use, bulls do not naturally

the best defense

head for red—they react to movement, not colors.

3 If the bull charges, remain still and then throw your shirt or hat away from you. The bull should head toward the moving object.

the best defense

CHAPTER 3

LEAPS OF
FAITH

HOW TO JUMP FROM A BRIDGE OR CLIFF INTO A RIVER

1 Jump feet-first.
Try to land in the channel—the deep water where boats go under the bridge. Stay away from any area with pylons that are supporting the bridge.

2 Keep your body completely vertical.

3 Squeeze your feet together.

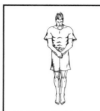

Jump feet-first in a vertical position; squeeze your feet together; clench your backside and protect your crotch.

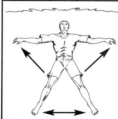

After you enter the water, spread your arms and legs wide and move them back and forth, which will slow your plunge. Attempt to slow your descent.

23. | leaps of faith

4 Enter the water feet-first, and clench your buttocks together.

If you do not, water may rush in and cause severe internal damage.

5 Protect your crotch area by covering it with your hands.

6 Immediately after you hit the water, spread your arms and legs wide and move them back and forth to generate resistance, which will slow your plunge to the bottom.

Always assume the water is not deep
enough to keep you from hitting bottom.

7 Swim to shore immediately after
surfacing.

leaps of faith

HOW TO MANEUVER ON TOP OF A MOVING TRAIN

1 Do not try to stand up straight (you probably will not be able to anyway). Stay bent slightly forward, leaning into the wind. If the train is moving faster than thirty miles per hour, it will be difficult to maintain your balance and resist the wind, so crawling on all fours may be the best method to get down.

2 If the train is approaching a turn, lie flat; do not try to keep your footing. If the car has guide rails along the edge, grab these and hold on.

3 If the train is approaching a tunnel entrance, lie flat, and quickly.

There is a bit of clearance between the top of a tunnel and the top of a train, but not enough room to stand. Do not assume that you can walk or crawl to the end of the car to get down and inside before you reach the tunnel— you probably won't.

27. *leaps of faith*

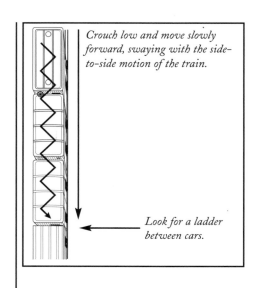

Crouch low and move slowly forward, swaying with the side-to-side motion of the train.

Look for a ladder between cars.

leaps of faith

4 | Move your body with the rhythm of the train—from side to side and forward.
Spread your feet about thirty-six inches apart as you wobble forward.

5 | Find the ladder at the end of the car (between two cars) and climb down.
It is very unlikely that there will be a ladder on the side of the car.

29. | *leaps of faith*

HOW TO JUMP FROM A MOVING CAR

1 Pull the emergency brake.
This may not stop the car, but it might slow it down enough to make jumping safer.

2 Open the car door.

3 Make sure you jump at an angle that will take you out of the path of the car. Tuck in your head, arms, and legs.

4 Aim for a soft landing site: grass, brush, wood chips, anything but pavement—or a tree.

Roll when you hit the ground.

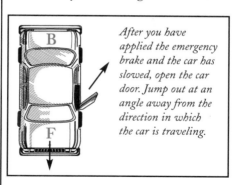

After you have applied the emergency brake and the car has slowed, open the car door. Jump out at an angle away from the direction in which the car is traveling.

31. *leaps of faith*

HOW TO LEAP FROM A MOTORCYCLE TO A CAR

1 Wear a high-quality helmet and a leather jacket plus leather pants and boots.

2 Make sure both vehicles are moving at the same speed.
The slower the speed, the safer the move. Anything faster than sixty miles per hour is extremely dangerous.

3 Wait for a long straight section of road.

4 Get the vehicles as close to each other as possible.

You will be on the passenger side of the car, so you will be very close to the edge of the roadway. Be careful not to swerve.

5 Stand crouched with both of your feet on either the running board or the seat.

33. *leaps of faith*

6 | Hold the throttle until the last instant.
Remember, as soon as you release the throttle the bike speed will decrease.

7 | If the car has a handle inside (above the door) grab it with your free hand. If not, simply time the leap so your torso lands in the car. If someone can grab you and pull you in, all the better.

8 | Have the driver swerve away from the bike as soon as you are inside.
Once you have released the handlebars,

the bike will go out of control and crash. This move is much easier with two people on the motorcycle so that the nonjumper can continue driving.

9 If you miss the window, tuck and roll away from the vehicles.

CHAPTER 4

EMERGENCIES

HOW TO IDENTIFY A MAIL BOMB

1 If a carrier delivers an unexpected bulky letter or parcel, inspect it for lumps or protrusions.

2 Handwritten labels or addresses on packages that supposedly come from companies are suspicious.
Watch for packages with missing or nonsensical return addresses.

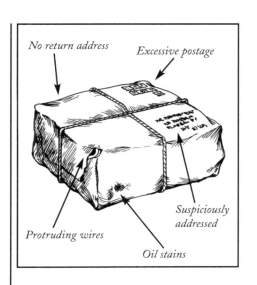

No return address

Excessive postage

Suspiciously addressed

Protruding wires

Oil stains

3 Watch out for excess postage on small packages or letters.
This indicates the object was not weighed by the post office.

4 Watch out for leaks, stains (especially oily stains), protruding wires, or excessive tape.

5 If you have good reason to believe it's a bomb, call 911.

HOW TO DELIVER A BABY IN A TAXICAB

1 Time the uterine contractions.
When contractions are about three to five minutes apart and last forty to ninety seconds—and increase in strength and frequency for at least an hour—the labor is most likely real.

2 As the baby moves out of the womb, its head—the biggest part of its body—will open the cervix so the rest of it can pass through.

41. *emergencies*

As the baby moves through the birth canal and out of the mother's body, guide it out by supporting the head and then the body.

3 When the baby is out of the mother, dry it off with a clean towel or shirt and keep it warm.
The baby will breathe on its own.
If necessary, clear any fluid out of the baby's mouth and nose with your fingers.

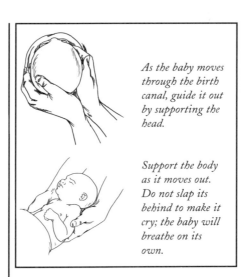

As the baby moves through the birth canal, guide it out by supporting the head.

Support the body as it moves out. Do not slap its behind to make it cry; the baby will breathe on its own.

4 Tie off the umbilical cord several inches from the baby using a piece of string or a shoelace.

Then leave it alone until you reach a hospital. If you are hours from a hospital, you can safely cut the cord by tying it in another place a few inches closer to the mother and cutting it between the knots. The placenta will follow in three to thirty minutes.

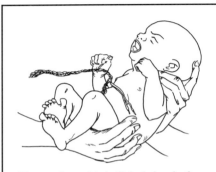

After you have dried off the baby, tie the umbilical cord with a shoelace or a piece of string several inches from the body. Leave the cord alone until the baby gets to the hospital.

45. | *emergencies*

HOW TO TREAT FROSTBITE

Frostbite is characterized by white, waxy skin that feels numb and hard. More severe cases result in a bluish-black skin color, and the most severe cases result in gangrene, which may lead to amputation. Frostbite should be treated by a doctor. However, in an emergency, take the following steps.

1 Remove wet clothing and dress the affected area with warm, dry clothing.

2 Immerse frozen areas in warm water (100 to 105°F) or apply warm compresses for ten to thirty minutes.

3 If warm water is not available, wrap gently in warm blankets.

4 Avoid direct heat, including electric or gas fires, heating pads, and hot water bottles.

5 Never thaw the area if it is at risk of refreezing; this can cause severe tissue damage.

HOW TO TREAT A LEG FRACTURE

1 If skin is broken, do not touch or put anything on the wound.
You must avoid infection. If the wound is severely bleeding, try to stop the flow of blood by applying steady pressure to the affected area with sterile bandages or clean clothes.

2 Do not move the injured leg—you need to splint the wound to stabilize the injured area.

48. *emergencies*

3 Find two stiff objects of the same length—wood, plastic, or folded cardboard—for the splints.

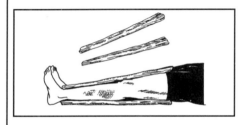

4 Put the splints above and under the injured area of the leg (or on the sides if moving the leg is too painful).

*You should be able
to slip one finger
under the rope, belt,
or fabric.*

5 Tie the splints with string, robe, or
belts—whatever is available.
Make sure the splint extends beyond
the injured area.

6 Do not tie the splints too tightly; this may cut off circulation.
If the splinted area becomes pale or white, loosen the ties.

7 Have the injured person lie flat on her back.
This helps blood continue to circulate and may prevent shock.

CHAPTER 5

ADVENTURE SURVIVAL

HOW TO SURVIVE IN THE LINE OF FIRE

1   Get as far away as possible.
An untrained shooter is not likely to be accurate at any distance greater than sixty feet.

2   Run fast, but do not move in a straight line—weave back and forth. The average shooter will not have the training necessary to hit a moving target at any real distance.

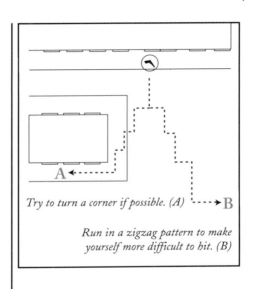

Try to turn a corner if possible. (A)

Run in a zigzag pattern to make yourself more difficult to hit. (B)

3 | Turn a corner if possible.

4 | Do not bother to count shots.
You will have no idea if the shooter
has more ammunition. Counting is
only for the movies.

HOW TO FIND WATER ON A DESERT ISLAND

1 Collect rainwater in whatever container is handy.

A bowl, plate, or helmet will work. So will a life raft and stretched clothing.

2 Collect dew.

Tie rags to your ankles and walk in grass or foliage at sunrise. Dew will gather on the material, which can then be wrung into a container.

Collect dew by tying rags to your ankles and walking at sunrise.

3 Catch fish.

The area around a fish's eye contains drinkable liquid, as do fish spines.

4 Look for bird droppings.
In arid climates, bird droppings
around a crack in a rock may indicate
a water source. Stuff a cloth into the
crack, then wring it out.

HOW TO SURVIVE AN EARTHQUAKE

1. If you are indoors, stay there.
Get under a desk or table and hang on
to it, or move into a doorway; the next
best place is in a hallway or against an
inside wall. Stay clear of windows, fire-
places, heavy furniture, or appliances.

2. If you are outside, get into the open,
away from buildings, power lines,
chimneys, or anything else that could
fall on you.

3 If you are driving, stop, but carefully. Move your car as far away from traffic as possible. Do not stop on or under a bridge, or under trees, light posts, or signs. Stay inside your car until the shaking stops.

4 If you are in a mountainous area, watch out for falling rocks, landslides, trees, and other debris that could be loosened by quakes.

adventure survival

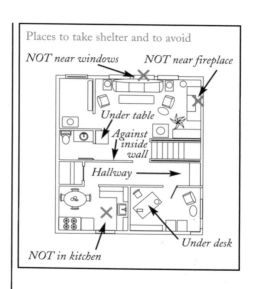

Places to take shelter and to avoid

NOT near windows

NOT near fireplace

Under table

Against inside wall

Hallway

NOT in kitchen

Under desk

5 After the quake stops, check for injuries and apply necessary first aid or seek help.

Do not attempt to move seriously injured persons unless they are in further danger of injury. Cover them with blankets and seek medical help for serious injuries.

6 If you can, put on a pair of sturdy thick-soled shoes (in case you step on broken glass, debris, etc.).

7 Check for hazards.

- Put out fires immediately.
- Shut off main gas valves only if you suspect a leak.
- Shut off power at the control box if there is any danger to house wiring.
- Do not touch downed utility lines.
- Clean up any harmful materials that may have spilled.
- Do not use a damaged chimney.
- Beware of shifted items when opening closets or cupboard doors.

8 Check food and water supplies.
Food in the freezer should be good for
at least a couple days. Avoid drinking
water from swimming pools and spas.

9 Be prepared for aftershocks.
Another quake, larger or smaller, may
follow.

HOW TO SURVIVE AN AVALANCHE

1 Struggle to stay on top of the snow by using a freestyle swimming motion.

2 If you are only partially buried, dig your way out with your hands or by kicking at the snow.

If you have a ski pole, poke through the snow until you feel open air.

3 If you are completely buried, dig a small hole around you and drool. The saliva will head down, telling you which direction is up. Dig up, and do it quickly.

HOW TO SURVIVE ADRIFT ON A LIFE RAFT

1 Take as many supplies from the ship as possible—especially water. Many canned foods, particularly vegetables, are packed in water, so take those if you can.

2 Protect yourself from the elements. You are more likely to die from exposure or hypothermia than of anything else.

3 Find food, if you can.

If your raft is floating for several weeks, seaweed will form on its underside and fish will naturally congregate in the shade beneath you.

4 If you see a plane or a boat nearby, try to signal it.

You can use these objects:

- Compass
- Watch
- Glasses
- Aluminum foil
- Aluminum can

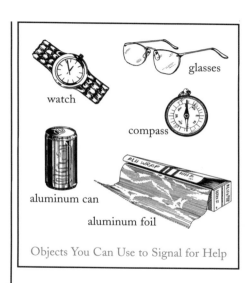

watch

glasses

compass

aluminum can

aluminum foil

Objects You Can Use to Signal for Help